CRACK AND COCAINE ABUSE

ALANA BENSON

Rosen
YA
New York

Published in 2019 by The Rosen Publishing Group, Inc.
29 East 21st Street, New York, NY 10010

First Edition

Library of Congress Cataloging-in-Publication Data

Names: Benson, Alana, author.
Title: Crack and cocaine abuse / Alana Benson.
Description: New York : Rosen Publishing, 2019 | Series: Overcoming addiction | Audience: Grades 7–12. | Includes bibliographical references and index.
Identifiers: LCCN 2017050367| ISBN 9781508179399 (library bound) | ISBN 9781508179566 (pbk.)
Subjects: LCSH: Cocaine abuse—Juvenile literature.
Classification: LCC RC568.C6 B46 2018 | DDC 613.8/4—dc23
LC record available at https://lccn.loc.gov/2017050367

Manufactured in the United States of America

CONTENTS

INTRODUCTION

If you or someone you know has an addiction, it can be painful and emotionally draining to endure. While not all addictions are the same, every addiction is harmful. Addictions to both cocaine and crack are damaging not only to the person suffering from the addiction, but to family and friends as well. Watching someone struggle with an addiction is devastating, but it is not without hope. The pain that comes with an addiction can become a memory rather than a way of life.

Cocaine and crack are both harmful drugs that are frequently grouped together. While they are related, they are not the same thing. They each have unique characteristics and histories. Cocaine is made from coca paste and hydrochloric acid and has existed since the late nineteenth century. Crack cocaine, more commonly just called crack, was invented much more recently, in the 1980s. Crack is made by mixing cocaine with baking soda and ammonia or water.

Cocaine is usually found in a white powder form, while crack typically looks like a white, tan, or light brown rock. Crack cocaine's name comes from the crackling noise the rocks make when they are heated. Both drugs are highly addictive and can

Learning about and dealing with addiction can be stressful, but dealing with the problem is much better than letting it get worse.

cause significant health problems. Cocaine can be injected, smoked, or snorted, and the way the drug is administered can manipulate how long its high is felt. Some users rub it on their gums, resulting in a tingling high.

When cocaine is injected or smoked, it takes between fifteen and thirty seconds before the high kicks in, but the high does not last long. When it is snorted, there is a longer delay before the user can start feeling its effects, generally around three to five minutes, but the resulting high lasts longer. This may not seem like a big difference to nonusers, but for someone who is addicted, the difference between minutes and seconds can feel like an eternity. Typically, injecting or smoking the drug means a shorter, more intense high while snorting it leads to a longer, less intense high.

Crack is almost exclusively smoked, and its effect is felt immediately. When crack rocks are heated, the vapors produce the smoke that is inhaled. The instant and intense high caused by this process is what makes crack so incredibly addictive. Modern street names for cocaine include coke, coca, cola, blanca, and snow white, among others. More common street names from the 1970s include movie star drug, studio fuel, love affair, and king's habit. Street names for crack include rocks, cookies, nuggets, and ice cubes. There are plenty of other street names for each drug that can vary depending on where you live. The street names for these drugs often illustrate their use, their social and cultural implications, and perceptions of the drug through time.

CHAPTER 1

RACE, CLASS, AND COKE

Before there was either cocaine or crack, there was the coca leaf. The coca leaf has been used by indigenous peoples in the Andean region, an area in modern-day Peru, for centuries. The coca leaf was, and still is today, chewed and brewed for tea. The coca leaf is a mild stimulant and suppresses hunger, thirst, pain, and fatigue. It can help cure altitude sickness, and many indigenous groups view it with sacred cultural significance.

The coca leaf can be processed into cocaine, which is why it has become a target of controversy, but the leaf has many other uses. It is important to remember that the coca leaf itself is harmless. In 1961, the United Nations (UN) added the coca leaf to a list of narcotics that it held to the same standards as drugs like cocaine and heroin. This effectively banned the leaf, stripping native groups in Peru, Bolivia, and other countries of

The coca leaf has many natural uses that the people of Peru, Bolivia, and other countries have used for centuries.

the right to cultivate the leaf for traditional uses. In 2013, Bolivia successfully petitioned the UN to include a clause that allows the chewing of coca leaves within a specific territory in their country.

A new strategy allows Bolivians to work with authorities in order to remove illegally grown coca plants. This strategy respects the people and culture the coca leaf is tied to, but also helps stem the tide of drug manufacturing. Working with the people in Bolivia is a tactic that appears to be more effective than the forced eradication of the plants, which continues in Peru.

DRUGS IN SODA?

Pharmacist John Pemberton created Coca-Cola in 1886 by mixing coca leaf extract with sugar syrup. He also used kola nut extract, giving the drink the second half of its name. After public opinion on the substance shifted from viewing it as a miracle medicine to a dangerous drug, the Coca-Cola company removed ecgonine (the alkaloid in the coca leaf used to make cocaine) from their recipe. By 1902, there was less than 1/400 of a gram of cocaine per ounce of syrup, but there were still trace amounts of cocaine present in the drink until 1929. These trace amounts were never enough to get drinkers high. Today, Coca-Cola is the only corporation allowed to import coca leaves into the United States under strict federal guidelines.

Advertisements like this one helped Coca-Cola and its mysterious recipe catapult to global fame.

FROM PLANT TO DRUG

In 1859, a German chemist named Albert Niemann extracted the active substance from coca leaves and named it cocaine. Cocaine was first used as a regional anesthetic, which means it could numb part of the body so doctors could perform medical procedures more easily on patients. By 1884, cocaine was viewed as a "miracle drug" and captured the attention of the medical community, including Dr. Sigmund Freud. Dr. Freud was a famous psychoanalyst, and he wrote several papers about the drug. He eventually developed an addiction to cocaine himself.

It was not until the early 1900s that people started realizing the dangers of cocaine. Hospitals and medical literature started reporting cases of nasal damage resulting from snorting cocaine. In 1912, there were 5,000 cocaine-related deaths, and ten years later, in 1922, cocaine was legally prohibited.

HOLLYWOOD'S FAVORITE DRUG

By the late 1800s, cocaine had a reputation as a fun, zany drug. Cocaine became popular as a subject matter in silent films and on set with actors as well. Cocaine helped actors stay awake and energetic during long days and made the antics of silent comedies appear more real.

After it was outlawed, cocaine use declined, that is, until the 1960s and '70s. These decades saw counterculture movements that questioned authority and the rules they put in place. Recreational drugs once again became popular. Some American universities saw a tenfold increase in cocaine use around this time. Cocaine's reputation changed as musicians, artists, and actors publicized their drug use. Pop culture, from rock music to

Even famous doctors like Sigmund Freud were in favor of cocaine at one point, until its effects became better understood.

movies, began helping spread the glamorous image of the "rich man's drug."

Between 1960 and 1999, hundreds of references to cocaine sprouted up. The Rolling Stones's "Cocaine Eyes" came out in 1970. The Eagles's hit "Life in the Fast Lane" came out in 1976, and Eric Clapton's cover of "Cocaine" was released in 1977. Quentin Tarantino's cult-classic film *Pulp Fiction* shows Uma Thurman snorting what she thinks is cocaine (but is actually heroin) and overdosing. The scene in *Scarface* that shows

Actor Al Pacino delivered a powerful performance as drug kingpin Tony Montana in the film *Scarface*.

exhausted cocaine kingpin Tony Montana collapsed in front of a mountain of cocaine has become iconic.

Certainly, cocaine has had a lasting impact on the art and music produced during the late twentieth century, but the works created during that time came at a price. There have been many deaths as a result of cocaine overdose, including many of the artists whose work celebrates the drug. Famous people whose deaths involved cocaine include John Belushi, Chris Farley, and Whitney Houston. Other celebrities such as writer Stephen King, singer Steven Tyler, actress Angelina Jolie, and supermodel Kate Moss have discussed their struggles with addiction to the drug and have received treatment.

THE "POOR MAN'S COCAINE"

Without cocaine there would be no crack. Crack was invented as a cheap alternative to cocaine and endured because of its instant and intense high. Crack cocaine first appeared in communities in Miami, and its production quickly spread to other major cities like New York City and Detroit. In 1982, one survey estimated that twenty-two million Americans had tried crack. Between 1984 and 1987, crack incidents jumped by almost 400 percent. The 1980s and 1990s saw a major spike in both drug use and crime, especially in impoverished areas. This became known as the crack epidemic. Studies of the crack epidemic as a period of history are highly contested because language referring to it often demonizes inner cities and minority populations.

In general, crack was less expensive and easier to access than cocaine, making it more prevalent in lower socioeconomic demographics than pure cocaine. The public perception became that cocaine was for wealthy artists, musicians, filmmakers,

President Barack Obama reduced the sentencing disparity for crack and cocaine possession in 2010 when he signed the Fair Sentencing Act into law.

and business tycoons, while crack lived in the impoverished neighborhoods of minorities. During the crack epidemic, African Americans were disproportionately targeted for drug crimes— and they still are today.

The fact that most crack users were white did not stop racially motivated incarcerations. The Anti-Drug Abuse Act of 1986 made possession of five grams of crack punishable by a five-year minimum jail sentence. For cocaine, one had to possess five hundred grams in order to reach the same sentence, meaning it took one hundred times as much cocaine as it did crack to earn the same punishment. This ruling, in addition to the intentional targeting of poor, mainly minority neighborhoods, resulted in the widespread prosecution and incarceration of African Americans, particularly men. By 2002, more than 80 percent of individuals charged with crack offenses were black, despite the fact that two-thirds of crack users were white.

These unjust laws endured until the passage of the Fair Sentencing Act of 2010, eliminating the five-year mandatory minimum sentence and increasing the amount of crack necessary to reach that sentence. Today, most people agree that race has nothing to do with whether or not the people of a community are more likely to do drugs. Growing up in poverty, facing violence, and the emotional and physical stress that often accompany these things are the prevailing factors that predict drug use.

CHAPTER 2

ARE YOU AT RISK?

The reason cocaine and crack are addictive is because they can make you feel really good—at least in the moment. Oftentimes, these periods of intense euphoria are followed by a strong crash of irritability, anxiety, and depression. You cannot have the highs of these drugs without the extreme lows, and the attempt to maintain that high is what leads to addiction. In order to avoid the crash, there is a natural urge to maintain the high, resulting in taking more and more of the drug, thus beginning the vicious cycle of addiction. Many people can try cocaine once and not become addicted. According to psychiatrist and drug researcher Dr. Carl Hart, only 10 to 20 percent of people who try it do become addicted. It is after the fourth or fifth time one gives in to the urge to continue the high that serious threats, like overdosing, can occur.

The only message many teens hear about drugs is "don't do them." People generally have a lot more questions that do not get answered. Often, teens try drugs because they can make

Using drugs is harmful to people at every age, but they are especially harmful to younger people. As a teenager, your brain is still developing and changing. Taking drugs can impact the growth of your mind.

Dr. Carl Hart is a doctor, scientist, and author. His work challenges long-held assumptions about drug use, addiction, and stereotypes.

Hart, a drug researcher at Columbia University, has debunked pre-existing studies that claim lab rats will uncontrollably consume cocaine if allowed. Hart's research shows that the rats will consume the drug in moderation as long as their environment provides other options, like food and sex. Hart nicely ties this experiment to the social conditions of the 1980s and 1990s:

> **Crack or any other drug isn't really all that overwhelmingly good or powerfully reinforcing: it gained the popularity that it achieved in the 'hood (far less than advertised) because there weren't that many other affordable sources of pleasure**

and purpose and because many of the people at the highest risk had other pre-existing mental illnesses that affected their choices. While drug use rates are similar across classes, addiction—like most other illnesses—is not an equal-opportunity disorder. Like cancer and heart disease, it disproportionately affects the poor, who have far less access to healthy diets and consistent medical care.

It is understood that cocaine and crack are dangerous and should not be abused. However, there does seem to be more room for research on exactly what "abusing" a drug means. This next phase of research might examine how poverty, a lack of proper stimulation and resources, education, and other factors, may have a bigger hand in addiction than just the drugs alone.

SIGNS OF ABUSE

With many addictions, it can be hard to find the line where a bad choice turns into a problem. With cocaine and crack, the line is typically clearer than with alcohol or marijuana. If you are unsure if you or someone you know is addicted to cocaine or crack, look for the following signs:

- **Frequent disappearances.** If someone is trying to keep up appearances of a normal life and hiding his or her addiction, that person will take any opportunity to leave a room to get a fix. If questioned, he or she may deflect or make a joke to make the continual absences seem like they're not a big deal.
- **Aggressive behavior.** Addictions may lead people to not act like themselves and to feel desperate to get their next fix. Standing in the way of that fix may lead to aggressive behavior,

Addictions can lead to aggressive behavior in those suffering from them, which might not be typical behavior for them otherwise.

like yelling, shoving, or abuse. Remember, if you are in any danger, get yourself to a safe place rather than trying to intervene in the addict's affairs.

- **Hyperactivity.** On cocaine, people may seem peppy and energetic. It can be easy to confuse this just for their personality, but when drugs are involved there is an edge to the energy that is not natural. If their energy seems more manic than natural, it may be a result of drug use.

Another sign that someone is using is that he or she is constantly looking for ways to pay for his or her habit, like borrowing money or gambling. Unless the individual is wealthy, going through large amounts of money could be a sign of addiction. Neither cocaine nor crack is a cheap habit. Prices vary depending on where it is bought but typically range from $120 to $150 or more for 1/8 ounce of cocaine. Crack may be cheaper, but users tend to use more of it, making the price comparable to what someone who uses cocaine with less regularity would spend. Street prices for crack tend to run at $50 to $60 per gram. For a regular user, using a handful of times during the day, the cost of crack runs about $225 a day.

It is difficult to calculate exactly how much more or less expensive crack is than cocaine. One 1997 study found that crack was not cheaper per pure unit than powder cocaine. Prices also vary depending on area and availability. In 2000, the Drug Enforcement Administration (DEA) found that prices for crack and cocaine were fairly similar in New Jersey, while in Chicago cocaine was much more expensive than crack. Pricing street drugs is tricky, as markets and values are always changing, but no matter what, both cocaine and crack are incredibly expensive habits.

MYTHS AND FACTS

MYTH: Cocaine gives you more energy, so it can make you better at your job or as an athlete.

FACT: While cocaine might give you more energy in the moment, that energy is often scattered and unproductive. You might not be focused enough to actually complete a task, or you might do it poorly. Cocaine use can harm your body, in turn making you a worse athlete. Drug use can also cost you your job or your place on a sports team simply by having it in your bloodstream.

MYTH: Crack is instantly and inevitably addicting

FACT: Both crack and cocaine are very addictive, but crack has often been more demonized than cocaine, with cocaine being viewed as more socially acceptable. Of those who have ever tried crack, 80 percent have not used it in the past year. A study from the *Journal of the American Medical Association* showed that crack cocaine is not significantly more addictive than powder cocaine. That being said, they are both addictive and dangerous, especially for younger people.

MYTH: "Everyone is doing it."

FACT: This is the easiest myth to bust. According to a study done by the Drug Policy Alliance in 2010, while 45 percent of twelfth graders stated that crack was easy to obtain, only 4 percent said they actually had tried it. As for cocaine, only 8 percent of high school seniors said they had tried it. In reality, not very many teenagers are using cocaine or crack.

CHAPTER 3

IS THE HIGH WORTH IT?

While on cocaine or crack, you can experience incredible highs. You might feel more confident than you ever have. If you suffer from anxiety, you might feel free of it for the first time, but only for a little while. The extreme highs of cocaine and crack come with extreme lows as well. Coming down from these drugs is so terrible that it can lead to addiction. When coming down from a high, you may experience some of the following:

- **Agitation and anxiety or other sudden, out-of-place changes in behavior.** While high, you may escape feelings of restlessness and anxiety, but when you come down, those feelings multiply.
- **Sickness.** As with other drugs, like alcohol, when you are recovering from the high, you may feel physically sick. You may experience nausea, muscle pain, and exhaustion. These are

Cocaine and crack can have significant side effects that make coming down from the high pretty miserable.

all symptoms of your body trying to regain balance within itself after being on these drugs.

- **Depression.** The intense joy and exhilaration that comes with being high can bring you down lower than before. Even if you do not suffer from depression, you could be opening yourself up to it during the period of coming down from the drug. Feeling like you can't get out of bed, not wanting to spend time with friends, and withdrawing from daily life are all symptoms of depression. Depression is common, and while it is not something to be ashamed of, it is not a way to go through life. If you are feeling depressed in general or as a result of personal or family drug use, reach out. There are ways to deal with depression, and it is worth getting help.

- **Risky sexual behavior.** Cocaine and crack might make sex feel better in the moment, but prolonged use can actually put a damper on your sex drive and make you lose desire for sex. In the beginning, with higher confidence and lower inhibitions, you may make decisions without thinking. In this state, it is easier to forget to use protection to prevent sexually transmitted diseases and pregnancy.
- **Insomnia, increased heart rate, hypertension (high blood pressure), and nosebleeds.**

As cocaine and crack are very similar drugs, many of their effects are the same. Some of the effects of crack in particular include cognitive decline, including a slower mental capacity and an inability to remember things; uncharacteristic irresponsibility; periods of high energy followed by periods of sleeplessness; being easily startled or nervous; physical shaking and low-grade fever; and incoherent speech. Physical signs of cocaine and crack abuse include cracked or blistered lips from smoking from a hot crack pipe; "crawling skin," or the sensation that bugs are crawling under your skin; dilated pupils; extreme weight loss; burns on fingers; coughing up phlegm; dry mouth; and a lack of personal hygiene. Long-term effects include sexual dysfunction and infertility, respiratory and kidney failure, stroke, and heart

IN HIS OWN WORDS

"I had been hooked for a year or two and I decided to kick it and I moved to France, which was the best thing I ever did. I cut all my connections to LA, had a new life and wrote Scarface *in an apartment in Paris. I wrote it straight which was good because I don't think cocaine helps writing. It's very destructive to the brain cells. I think my writing was getting shallower."*

—*Oliver Stone, the screenwriter of* Scarface *on quitting cocaine.*

Screenwriter and director Oliver Stone quit using cocaine in order to write the screenplay that would become *Scarface*.

attack. Many people have died from these as a result of long-term cocaine or crack addiction.

DANGERS OF OVERDOSING

According to the National Center for Health Statistics, 5,856 people died from cocaine overdose in 2014. In 2015, 6,986 people died. In 2016, the death tally for cocaine overdoses was 10,619. The drugs themselves do not cause a person to die, but the reaction within the body does. Most deaths occur because the drugs contribute to heart attacks, strokes, seizures, or other medical problems that can lead to death.

Some of the signs of overdose are similar to the signs that someone is high on cocaine or crack. If you have any doubt that you or someone else is overdosing, call 911, because it could save your or that person's life. Some changes in vital signs that might indicate an overdose include:

- Abnormally high blood pressure
- Irregular heart rate
- Extremely high body temperature
- Increased respiration (breathing rate)
- Changes in pulse

Other symptoms include extreme anxiety, confusion, or disorientation; hallucinations or psychosis; nausea or vomiting; agitation or tremors; clammy skin; chest pains; diarrhea; difficulty urinating; and unconsciousness.

After calling 911, there are some things you can do to help the person while you wait for medical assistance. If the person is having a seizure and is standing, attempt to gently hug the person and help him or her onto the ground, preferably on his or her side so the person cannot choke on his or her saliva. Move any furniture the person could injure himself or herself on out of the way. Do not attempt to put anything into the person's mouth, as he or she could bite your finger or chip a tooth. Let the person seize: if you try to hold him or her down, he or she could dislocate a shoulder. After the seizure, the best thing to do is to keep that individual calm. Elevating his or her heart rate with panic can make those symptoms worse. When assisting someone who is overdosing, if you stay calm, it may help the victim stay calm as well. It can be terrifying to watch someone go through an overdose, but maintaining a cool head may help you save his or her life.

Staying calm is critical if you think you are overdosing. Keep your heart rate as low as possible and dial 911. Keeping your heart rate low slows the process and may prevent further harm.

CHAPTER 4

WHERE LAW ENFORCEMENT AND TREATMENT COLLIDE

In 1971, President Nixon declared a War on Drugs. Drug use had increased through the sixties and had become a symbol of rebellion, social activism, and political dissent. The government stopped research on how drugs work in people and their safety and focused more on stopping drug use altogether. The policies put in place at this time led to more drug control agencies, mandatory sentencing, and no-knock warrants. Years afterward, when asked about the War on Drugs, a top Nixon aide admitted:

We knew we couldn't make it illegal to be either against the [Vietnam] war or black people, but by getting the public

to associate the hippies with marijuana and blacks with heroin, and then criminalizing both heavily, we could disrupt those communities. We could arrest their leaders, raid their homes, break up their meetings, and vilify them night after night on the evening news. Did we know we were lying about the drugs? Of course we did.

The War on Drugs has not gone well and has caused a great deal of harm. Drug use rates are up across the entire country, and the ramifications of the War on Drugs have left lasting scars. According to the Drug Policy Alliance, from 1980 to 1997, the number of individuals incarcerated for nonviolent drug offenses increased from 50,000 to more than 400,000. During Ronald Reagan's presidency in the 1980s, First Lady Nancy Reagan started the "Just Say No" campaign. This

It has been common practice to treat drug use and addiction as a crime. However, critics of the practice argue that users who are punished with jail time do not get the treatment they need.

US government initiative told kids to "just say no" to drug use. Many critics of the campaign have stated that it oversimplified the complexity of drug use and made it harder for drug users to seek help. This period saw unfounded fears about drug use and drug users skyrocket. Many people who needed help or therapy ended up in jail or on the street.

STRUGGLING WITH STIGMA

Drugs and the people who use them face severe societal pressure. Due in part to the War on Drugs, the stigma of drug use and those struggling with addictions is harsh. Advertising campaigns that vilified drug use, rather than looking at addiction as a disease, made users feel that their addictions were something to be ashamed of. Many people—especially teenagers—still feel that they cannot talk about their drug use without getting in trouble. Most students do not feel comfortable going to their health teacher or guidance counselor to talk about drugs, especially if they have already used them. The fear of getting in trouble is enough to make kids not want to speak with authority figures— they would rather get their information from their friends or the internet.

Aside from the fear of getting in trouble, the fear of stigma looms large. Drug use comes with many stereotypes. Even in 2016, a well-known American politician stated, "Good people don't smoke marijuana." If this is the message coming from our political leaders, that you cannot be a good person if you do drugs or have done them in the past, how could anyone feel comfortable coming forward to talk about it? Asking for help is hard enough as it is, especially when it comes to talking about

This Place CLOSED

For Violation of the National Prohibition Act

BY ORDER OF

U. S. DISTRICT COURT

Prohibition in the 1920s outlawed alcohol. Prohibition created speakeasies and gangs that made money by illegally importing and selling alcohol. How has prohibiting drugs affected drug use?

addiction. Many people see addiction as a weakness rather than a disease and are judgmental, thinking that drug use is due to a character flaw. Plenty of good people have used drugs, continue to use drugs, and suffer from drug addictions. Using drugs like cocaine and crack does not hurt your character or make you a bad person, but these drugs can hurt your body, your mind, and your relationships.

FACT VERSUS FICTION: " CRACK BABIES"

Many myths and legends surround the crack epidemic, and only recently have journalists and historians taken a closer look at the roots of these stories. During the height of the War on Drugs, the media seized onto certain aspects of crack in order to vilify users. In particular, the use of the term "crack babies," meaning infants who were born to mothers who had used crack or cocaine during their pregnancies, became widespread in the media. The theories at the time about the conditions of these babies and the damage done to them were based on very small, inaccurate studies. At that time, many people believed that not only would these babies be born addicted to crack, but they would also face enormous obstacles integrating into normal life. The media projected a future of a drug-addled society filled with crack-derived mental and physical handicaps.

New studies that have followed the lives of these so-called crack babies have shown the opposite to be true. Most individuals who were born to mothers who used crack have led perfectly normal, healthy lives. They do not suffer from drug addiction in droves and, in some cases, knowing their family history of addiction can make them more cautious in regard to drug abuse. Dr. Hallam Hurt conducted one of these studies between 1989 and 1992. Dr. Hurt followed the babies of mothers who had smoked crack during their pregnancies and found that "there were no differences in the health and life outcomes between babies exposed to crack and those who weren't." What she did notice, however, was that poverty and violence were the factors that made a difference in the lives of those children

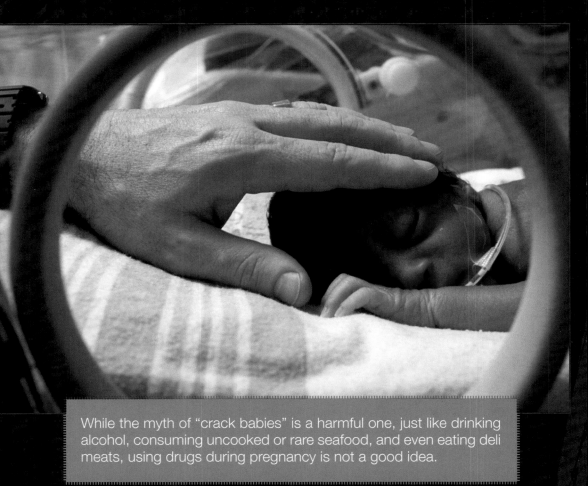

While the myth of "crack babies" is a harmful one, just like drinking alcohol, consuming uncooked or rare seafood, and even eating deli meats, using drugs during pregnancy is not a good idea.

While the myth of the "crack baby" spiraled out of control, using crack or cocaine while pregnant can create medical problems for both the mother and child. Using cocaine during the first few months of a pregnancy can increase the risk of miscarriage and also increases the risk that the child will have reduced growth potential and some physical defects, though many of these defects can be outgrown provided the child receives sufficient care and nutrition. Providing care and treatment options for pregnant women suffering from a drug addiction is the most effective way of ensuring the health of both the mother and child. Incarcerating pregnant women who use crack or cocaine is the least effective way of caring for them.

PROHIBITING PROHIBITION

Instead of using law enforcement to stop people from committing violent acts against each other, the War on Drugs and the way drug users were criminalized made law enforcement stop a person from committing violence against themselves. It turned a public health issue into a crime. Many critics of the War on Drugs state that putting a drug user in jail (where there is plenty of access to drugs) and then releasing that person with a criminal record helps no one and makes law enforcement more difficult. This leads to lots of "criminals" with no options, who can then be easily lead back to a life of drug use or even drug dealing.

Today, new ideas about handling drug use are circulating, and some are being put into practice. New legalization laws in Colorado and Washington allow marijuana to be regulated, sold, and taxed for various purposes. A police group called Law Enforcement Action Partnership (LEAP) calls for legalizing drugs and cites the prohibition of alcohol in the 1920s—and the skyrocketing of homicide rates and the criminal enterprises that sprang from it—as evidence of why drugs should not be so tightly regulated. These groups are lobbying for a change in how drug convictions are handled—with treatment, not jail.

UNBIASED DRUG DATA

It is very difficult to find unbiased data when it comes to drugs. Drug use and abuse is such a controversial topic that sources sometimes pick and choose their statistics to fit their message. Making sure your source is unbiased will help you find more

Many critics of the War on Drugs state that it turned a public health issue into a crime.

accurate drug data. Exploring biased sides of the issue is important, too, and it might even change your opinion. Since the height of the War on Drugs, drug policy has begun to shift from fear mongering to sensible, treatment-based policy. Instead of looking at people who struggle with addiction with contempt, now many people understand all the complicated factors that come with addictions, like poverty, family history, violence, and mental illness. Today, many people realize that sympathy and kindness are far better medicines than hatred and fear for those who suffer from drug addictions.

CHAPTER 5

HOW TO GET HELP

A common adage used by drug and alcohol recovery groups is "the first step to recovery is admitting you have a problem." It can be extremely difficult to admit to suffering from an addiction or to point out a loved one's addiction. It can take years of difficult living before someone realizes he or she needs to make a change. Sometimes a partner has to threaten to leave or does leave. Maybe a driving under the influence (DUI) conviction means rock bottom. Whatever the moment is, the time leading up to it can be excruciating for everyone. Watching someone you love deal with an addiction is heartbreaking. You worry for that person's well-being constantly, while still trying to take your own into account. But at what point is enough enough? At what point do you walk away from someone you love if he or she refuses your help? These questions are difficult for the loved one of someone dealing with an addiction to ask himself or herself and hard for the addict to hear.

Helping a loved one overcome an addiction can lead to a happier, healthier life for everyone. Recovery is difficult, but it is possible.

Do not beat yourself up. Addiction is a brain disorder and something to which you may have a predisposition. Addictions are no one's fault. Even having the ability to self-reflect on an addiction, whether yours or a loved one's, is an important step in the process of recovering. If you are using drugs like crack or cocaine, be proud that you have the self-awareness to take steps to recovery and know that you can recover. Nothing about this process is easy, but it is possible. If you think you or a loved one might have an addiction to cocaine or crack, your first step is to take stock. Are you safe? Are you in a position to seek out help? If you are in an abusive relationship with your loved one, be sure you put yourself in a safe place first, maybe staying with a friend or at a shelter, before attempting to get treatment for him or her.

Coming to terms with an addiction and deciding to make a change is a huge first step. The emotional upset that can come with these realizations is not to be understated. Make sure you or your loved one gets adequate support. This could mean a range of things, from seeing a therapist, to talking to a friend, to checking into a rehabilitation center. Think of all those options as different levels of support. Unlike in the past, we understand that the path to healing does not include demonizing. Do not feel afraid to reach out for help because that is the only way to start. Addictions are incredibly difficult to live with, and they only get more difficult when you deal with them alone.

If your loved one is struggling, make sure that you support him or her and that you find some support yourself. It is unsustainable to be a crutch to a person struggling with addiction, so make sure you also have an outlet where you can talk about your frustrations and your fears. Spend time with people who support the decision to stay clean; spending time with old friends with whom you or your loved one did drugs can be detrimental to recovery and might lead to a relapse.

TREATMENT APPROACHES

There are several treatment approaches for quitting cocaine or crack—from "going cold turkey," which means quitting immediately, to slower forms of rehabilitation. Behavioral treatments and pharmacological ones can both be effective and are often used in combination with each other. Pharmacological, or medical, treatments are still in research phases. A cocaine vaccine and various other medications are being developed, but they are still in the testing phases and are not yet approved for general use. Medical researchers are also looking at treatments to help with the emergencies that arise from cocaine overdose.

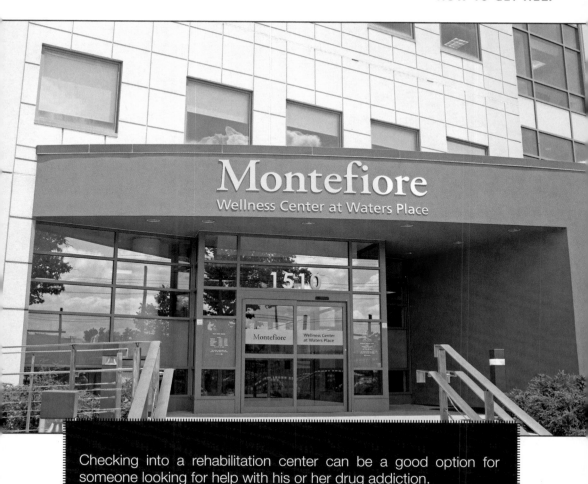

Checking into a rehabilitation center can be a good option for someone looking for help with his or her drug addiction.

Hopefully, these clinical trials will end up widening the spectrum of therapy and the treatments available. Until then, however, there are other medical options to help through the difficulties of withdrawal. Antianxiety medications have helped some recovering cocaine addicts, and neurostimulation has shown potential for crack addiction treatment.

One type of behavioral therapy is called contingency management (CM). This treatment involves using motivational

Talking with a therapist is a good way for a loved one of an addict to find an outlet to talk about her experience.

incentives to reward good, drug-free behavior. If a patient has a drug-free urine test, for example, he or she might be rewarded with things that encourage healthy lifestyles, like points toward a gym membership or vouchers to buy a new outfit. According to the National Institute on Drug Abuse, CM can be particularly helpful for patients to "achieve initial abstinence from cocaine and stay in treatment," especially when used in community treatment programs.

Cognitive-behavioral therapy (CBT) helps people recognize patterns within their addictions that can lead to relapse. This includes learning what scenarios are most likely to make a person want use drugs and then avoiding them. If someone with an addiction always used to use cocaine at parties, this therapy would help the user identify his or her patterns and then make choices that would not put himself or herself in the partylike scenarios in which he or she would be more tempted to use cocaine.

These treatments can be implemented in individual therapy sessions, during which a user sees a therapist while living at home and going about his or her daily life, or as part of inpatient treatment, where people can stay for a period of a month or more in rehabilitation centers and receive therapy and addiction-recovery support.

HOW EXPENSIVE IS REHAB?

The thought of checking into a rehabilitation program can deter some people who are struggling with addiction. The cost of rehab is no small thing; many rehab programs run upwards of $20,000 to $30,000. Fortunately, most insurance plans will cover the cost of rehab.

If you do not have insurance, however, the options are a little different. This is particularly troubling when you remember that individuals living in poverty are more likely to abuse drugs and often do not have a strong support system behind them.

If you do not have insurance and cannot afford inpatient treatment, you can still take part in outpatient treatment programs. Outpatient programs include groups like Narcotics Anonymous, in which you live at home, go to work or school, and attend meetings at night or on weekends to help you with recovery. Narcotics Anonymous holds almost 67,000 meetings weekly in 139 countries. Their treatment approach uses a twelve-step program. Members attend group meetings to support and talk to each other. They intentionally chose the name Narcotics Anonymous because they did not want to differentiate between the use of any particular drug—addicts of all kinds are welcome, and membership is totally free. Narcotics Anonymous is a great first step if you are dealing with an addiction of any kind, whether or not you can afford rehab. Many people who begin treatment through Narcotics Anonymous continue to take part in meetings for many years, even when they have been in recovery for long periods of time.

WHAT TO EXPECT WHEN RECOVERING FROM ADDICTION

Recovering from cocaine and crack addictions is difficult and painful. The next step after recognizing you have a problem and seeking treatment is detoxification. This process cleans the drug out of the user's body. During detox, the following symptoms can occur for both cocaine and crack withdrawal: intense cravings for the drug, anxiety, severe depression, insomnia and fatigue, and nightmares. Detox is the first step before beginning to live a life in which you are not under the influence of drugs.

Unfortunately, relapse is a real possibility that many recovering addicts face. Relapse occurs when someone has committed to not taking drugs and then falls back into the pattern of using. Relapse does not mean you or your loved one has failed, and it does not mean you or your loved one cannot recover. Relapsing is especially common when something tragic in the user's life occurs, such as the death of a loved one, the reestablishing of old patterns and friendships, or dealing with a recurrent mental illness like depression. If you or your loved one relapses, support is especially important.

Addiction to and recovery from any drug is a lifelong commitment. Many former addicts attest to the fact that some days are good and some days are bad. Sometimes they really want to get high or drunk, but emphasizing the good parts of their lives and what they can achieve precisely because they are clean helps them commit to staying drug free every day. There are many resources for help at any point along the journey to living a drug-free life, whether it is day one or day one thousand.

The important thing to remember is that while someone may struggle with an addiction for the rest of his or her life, that person does not have to spend his or her life addicted. Many addicts of both cocaine and crack have made choices that have changed their lives for the better. It may feel hopeless now, but this is not a permanent state. Change is an option, and you are not alone. Finding others who have recovered or who have helped a loved one recover can help. They can be a guide for you along the path. If you need to connect with someone who understands what it is like to love someone who is addicted to drugs, Nar-Anon is for friends and family of addicts and can serve as an excellent resource. In the words of an addict in the process of recovery, "pain is becoming a memory." For you, too, pain can be a part of your past and not necessarily a part of your future.

TEN GREAT QUESTIONS
TO ASK A DRUG-ADDICTION COUNSELOR

1. How do crack and cocaine hurt people?

2. How can I help my friend if he or she has an addiction?

3. What are some strategies to turn down drugs?

4. How do cocaine and crack affect peoples' brains?

5. How has the war on drugs affected teenagers?

6. Alcohol and coffee are legal, so why aren't other drugs?

7. What should I look for in a drug-treatment program?

8. How does therapy work?

9. Does mental illness, like depression or anxiety, affect drug use?

10. How do I know if I'm addicted?

GLOSSARY

ADDICTION A brain disorder in which an individual cannot stop using a substance through his or her own volition.

ANTI-DRUG ABUSE ACT A 1986 law that made having five grams of crack punishable by five years of prison—the same consequences as five hundred grams of cocaine. This created a racial and class division between prosecutions of drug crimes.

COCA A plant grown in Bolivia and Peru that indigenous peoples have chewed and used in teas for centuries.

COCAINE An addictive drug made from coca paste and hydrochloric acid in the form of a white powder.

CRACK COCAINE An addictive drug, also known simply as crack made from cocaine and a mixture of other ingredients including baking soda, ammonia, and water. It is usually found in rock form with a brownish-white color.

CRACK EPIDEMIC A contentious time period during the 1980s and '90s when crack cocaine use was highlighted by the media. The media hype on crack use expanded racial inequalities and divides and imprisoned thousands.

CULTIVATE To raise or grow plants, particularly for commercial purposes.

DEMONIZE To portray someone as evil, dangerous or threatening.

DEPRESSION A mental disorder that affects how an individual feels and thinks and can cause feelings of hopelessness and a lack of desire to be present in his or her life.

ECGONINE The naturally occurring alkaloid in the coca leaf used to process cocaine.

EUPHORIA A state of intense happiness or excitement.

IMPOVERISHED Extremely poor.

INDIGENOUS The native people, plants, or animals of a region.

PROHIBITION A form of law that completely outlaws a certain thing, i.e. alcohol prohibition in the 1920s.

RELAPSE When someone has committed to stop taking drugs but falls back into the pattern of using again.

STIGMA A mark of disgrace or shame on a person or action, designated by cultural norms and opinions.

STIMULANT A substance that increases the user's excitement and energy.

WAR ON DRUGS The period started by former president Richard Nixon in which drugs were completely outlawed and were viewed with a zero-tolerance policy. Police became militarized, addicts were imprisoned, and drug dealers were punished with severe jail sentences.

WITHDRAWAL The painful physical and mental process an individual dealing with an addiction goes through when he or she stops using drugs.

FOR MORE INFORMATION

Addiction Center

Recovery Worldwide LLC

121 South Orange Avenue, Suite 1450

Orlando, FL 32801

(888) 978-3383

Email: contact@addictioncenter.com

Website: https://www.addictioncenter.com

Facebook: @TheAddictionCenter

Founded in 2014, the Addiction Center is a web-based resource that connects addicts with treatment centers. Addiction Center is run by Recovery Worldwide, a company that owns several treatment facilities around the United States. The website also publishes informative articles on addiction and recovery.

Canada Drug Rehab

Sunshine Coast Health Centre

2174 Fleury Road

Powell River, BC V8A 0H8

Canada

(877) 746-1963

Website: http://www.canadadrugrehab.ca

This web search tool helps drug users search for local treatment facilities and meetings in Canada. The site includes searches for drug recovery options and allows users to search for programs that will meet their individual recovery and economic needs.

Canadian Centre on Substance Use and Addiction (CCDUS)
75 Albert Street, Suite 500
Ottawa, ON K1P 5E7
Canada
(613) 235-4048
Website: http://www.ccdus.ca
Twitter: @CCSACanada
This website of this organization lists phone numbers for specific regions within Canada that can then direct callers to resources for substance abuse. The website also outlines most drugs and topics related to them. The organization supports evidence-based research on the topic of addiction.

Drug Policy Alliance
131 West 33rd Street, 15th Floor
New York, NY 1001
(212) 613-8020
Website: http://www.drugpolicy.org
Email: NYC@drugpolicy.org
Facebook: @drugpolicy
Twitter: @DrugPolicyOrg
The Drug Policy Alliance's mission is to advance and support policies in which the "use and regulation of drugs are grounded in science, compassion, health and human rights." They support reducing the criminalization of drugs and promote health-centered drug policy. Their website features factual, nonpolitical drug information and lots of resources.

Narcotics Anonymous (NA)
PO Box 9999
Van Nuys, CA 91409

(818) 773-9999
Website: https://www.na.org
Email: fsmail@na.org
Narcotics Anonymous offers free outpatient therapy in a group
    setting. If you or a loved one is struggling with an addiction,
    finding a meeting near you on the NA website could be a
    great first step to recovery.

National Institute on Drug Abuse (NIDA)
6001 Executive Boulevard
Room 5213, MSC 9561
Bethesda, MD 20892
(301) 443-1124
Website: https://www.drugabuse.gov
Facebook: @NIDANIH
Twitter: @NIDAnews
This science-based organization is dedicated to doing research
    on all aspects of drug use. They wish to spread public
    awareness of addiction as a brain disorder.

Substance Abuse and Mental Health Services Administration
    (SAMHSA)
.5600 Fishers Lane
Rockville, MD 20857
(800) 487-4889
Website: https://www.samhsa.gov
Facebook: @Samhsa
Twitter: @Samhsagov
SAMHSA is a national organization committed to finding mental
    health and addiction help for those in need. SAMHSA has a
    grant program and has the ability to help lower-income
    individuals and families get the help they need.

FOR FURTHER READING

Ambrose, Marylou, and Veronica Deisler. *Investigate Cocaine and Crack*. New York, NY: Enslow Publishing, 2015.

Engle, Charlie. *Running Man*. New York, NY: Simon & Schuster Ltd, 2016.

Hamilton, Tracy Brown. *I Am Addicted to Drugs. Now What? (Teen Life 411)*. New York, NY: Rosen Publishing, 2017.

Hart, Carl L. *High Price: A Neuroscientist's Journey of Self-Discovery That Challenges Everything You Know about Drugs and Society*. New York, NY: Harper, 2013.

Latchana, Kenney K. *The Hidden Story of Drugs*. New York, NY: Rosen Digital, 2014.

McKenzie, Precious. *Helping a Friend with a Drug Problem*. New York, NY: Rosen Publishing, 2017.

Orr, Tamra. *The Truth About Cocaine*. New York, NY: Rosen Publishing, 2014.

Scott, Celicia. *Hard Drugs: Cocaine, LSD, PCP, & Heroin*. Broomall, PA : Mason Crest, 2015.

Watkins, D. *The Cook Up: A Crack Rock Memoir*. New York, NY: Grand Central Publishing, 2016.

Wensley, Clarkson. *Cocaine Confidential*. London, UK: Quercus, 2014.

BIBLIOGRAPHY

Barbier, Chrystelle. "Bolivia Resists Global Pressure to Do Away with Coca Crop." *Guardian*, April 24, 2015. http://www.theguardian.com/world/2015/apr/24/bolivia-coca-growing-cocaine.

Barron, James. "Use of Cocaine, but Not Other Drugs, Seen Rising." *New York Times*, September 29, 1986. http://www.nytimes.com/1986/09/29/nyregion/use-of-cocaine-but-not-other-drugs-seen-rising.html.

Benson, Alana. "Interview with *Narconon* Representative." Narconon. Conducted September 21, 2017.

Blickman, Tom. "Coca Leaf: Myths and Reality." *Transnational Institute*, August 5, 2014. https://www.tni.org/en/primer/coca-leaf-myths-and-reality.

Bowser, Betty Anne. "Cocaine: How 'Miracle Drug' Nearly Destroyed Sigmund Freud, William Halsted." *PBS NewsHour*, October 17, 2011.http://www.pbs.org/newshour/bb/health-july-dec11-addiction_10-17.

Choices Recovery. "What Happens If Crack Cocaine Is Abused During Pregnancy?" January 20, 2016. http://crehab.org/blog/information/what-happens-if-crack-is-abused-during-pregnancy.

Forever Recovery, A. "Are Athletes Using Cocaine as a Performance Enhancer." November 13, 2015. http://aforeverrecovery.com/blog/drugs/is-cocaine-used-as-a-performance- enhancer-by-athletes.

Hart, Carl L. "As With Other Problems, Class Affects Addiction." *New York Times*, March 10, 2014. https://www.nytimes.com

/roomfordebate/2014/02/10/what-is-addiction/as-with-other
-problems-class-affects-addiction.

Ingraham, Christopher. "Trump's Pick for Attorney General: 'Good People Don't Smoke Marijuana.'" *Washington Post*, November, 18, 2016. https://www.washingtonpost.com /news/wonk/wp/2016/11/18/trumps-pick-for-attorney -general-good-people-dont-smoke-marijuana/?utm _term=.3afa8bfaa883.

Krishnan, Manisha. "We Asked Drug Addicts How Much Their Habit Costs Them." *Vice*, March 18, 2016. https://www.vice .com/en_us/article/nn9p3k/the-cost-of-being-a-drug -addict-in-canada.

Leonard, Kimberly. "These Are the Drugs Killing the Most People in the U.S." *U.S. News & World Report*, December 20, 2016. https://www.usnews.com/news/articles/2016-12-20 /heroin-cocaine-among-top-drug-killers-in-us.

LoBianco, Tom. "Report: Aide says Nixon's War on Drugs Targeted Blacks, Hippies." CNN, March 24, 2016. http://www .cnn.com/2016/03/23/politics/john-ehrlichman-richard -nixon-drug-war-blacks-hippie/index.html

National Geographic Channel. "Drugs, Inc. Facts: Crack." December 9, 2011. http://channel.nationalgeographic.com /drugs-inc/articles/drugs-inc-facts-crack.

Okie, Susan. "Crack Babies: The Epidemic That Wasn't." *New York Times*, January 26, 2009. https://www.nytimes .com/2009/01/27/health/27coca.html.

Project Know: Understanding Addiction. "Cocaine Overdose." February 26, 2013. https://www.projectknow.com/ research /cocaine-overdose.

Reed, Todd. "Former Crack Baby: 'It's Another Stigma, Another Box to Put Me In'." *Al Jazeera America*, March 10, 2015. http://

america.aljazeera.com/watch/shows/america-tonight/articles/2015/3/10/crack-baby-myth.html.

Reinarman, Craig. "5 Myths About That Demon Crack." *Washington Post*, October 14, 2007. http://www.washingtonpost.com/wp-dyn/content/article/2007/10/09/AR2007100900751.html.

Sullum, Jacob. "Everything You've Heard About Crack And Meth Is Wrong." *Forbes*, November 4, 2013. https://www.forbes.com/sites/jacobsullum/2013/11/04/everything-youve-heard-about-crack-and-meth-is-wrong.

Total Film. "The Total Film Interview—Oliver Stone." November 1, 2003. http://www.gamesradar.com/the-total-film-interview-oliver-stone.

U.S. Drug Enforcement Administration. "DEA History Book, 1985-1990." August 23, 2006. https://web.archive.org/web/20060823024931/http://www.usdoj.gov/dea/pubs/history/1985-1990.html

INDEX

building achievements."

Introduction

Throughout the world today there are many examples of incredible architectural achievements. Many of these magnificent structures were designed and built hundreds, sometimes thousands, of years ago without the benefit of modern technology and often under difficult and primitive conditions.

Think about this ... you're the project manager for a large company that designs theme parks. In your budget you have 500 million dollars to build any **one** of the six building projects in this book! Your task is to decide which one your company will construct for the theme park.

But there's a catch! You have to build the replica exactly the way the original was built!

Join the author on an imaginary flight to these six countries — the USA, Scotland, England, France, Egypt, and India — to research how six famous structures were designed and built.

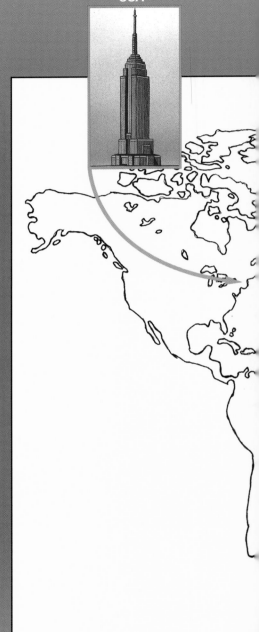

Empire State Building, USA

4

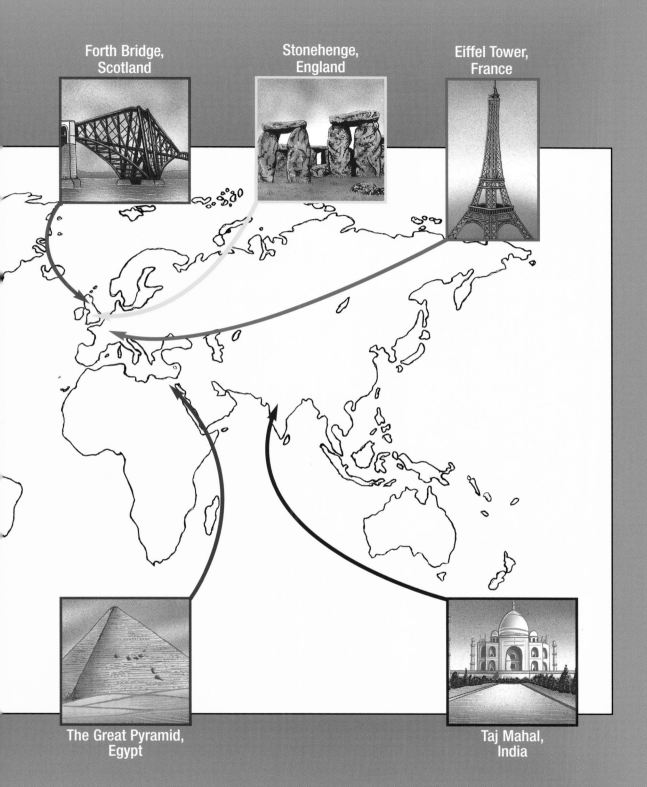

Forth Bridge,
Scotland

Stonehenge,
England

Eiffel Tower,
France

The Great Pyramid,
Egypt

Taj Mahal,
India

1. How to Build the Great Pyramid

The Great Pyramid is an ideal structure to consider building as it has a low difficulty rating. But … it will need a large amount of land and it will take a long time to build. After you have read the information sections "What You Will Need" and "The Building Method," estimate how much quicker you and your construction team could build it today.

On Strike!

Pyramid building was expensive — and sometimes workers were not paid or fed on time. The world's first "strike" was recorded around 3,000 years ago when men building a pharaoh's tomb were not given enough food. The pharaoh, eager to get his tomb finished, agreed to the builders' demands!

6

History: The Great Pyramid

For more than 4,500 years, people have marveled at the original Great Pyramid in Egypt. Some people think the Great Pyramid was built as a tomb for the Egyptian Pharaoh, Cheops. Others think that it was built as a huge observatory for the stars. At the time it was built, most people lived in buildings made from dried mud bricks, reeds, and small stones. The designers of the Great Pyramid wanted to build something larger and more magnificent than anyone had ever seen before. And, they did.

What You Will Need

Location: To build an authentic Great Pyramid, you would need a large, sandy area with plenty of space. A square area, about 250 yards long and 250 yards wide, will be fine.

Make sure that the area doesn't have any soggy ground or soft rocks underneath, as the pyramid will end up weighing over 6,000,000 tons. The theme park company would not want their Great Pyramid to sink into the ground!

Materials: You would need about 2,500,000 large square blocks of stone, each of them weighing about 2.5 tons. As you have to build the pyramid in exactly the same way as the ancient Egyptians, it would be cheating to move the stones using vehicles with wheels. Instead, you would need lots of tree trunks to roll the blocks over, and as much rope as you can find.

Tools: You would need hard sharp stones, some bronze tools, and wooden implements.

Workers: At least 100,000 workers would be needed to complete an authentic pyramid. Most of them would be employed to move the blocks of stone into place. You would also need stonemasons, stone carvers, painters, and engineers.

Time: A Great Pyramid, using authentic tools and methods, would take about 20 years to build.

Mummies

Inside pyramids and other tombs, the ancient Egyptians preserved the bodies of their dead as "mummies" so they did not rot or decay. Dead bodies had their internal organs removed and stored in jars. Then they were covered in salt and special bandages to dry them out. After drying, bodies were covered with oil, filled with linen, and tightly wrapped in more bandages. For each body, the process took about 70 days.

The Building Method

Step 1: You would start your pyramid by using stone hammers to dig tunnels into the rock underneath where the pyramid will be. These tunnels will lead to the burial chamber, where any pharaohs that you wish to bury may be hidden.

Step 2: Next, you would carefully measure out where the four corners of your pyramid are going to be, and haul the first four blocks of your pyramid into place. Only 2,499,996 to go! You must make sure you get them in exactly the right position, though. If you make a mistake, you'll have to haul all the stone blocks off your pyramid and start over again.

TIP! To be authentic, the hardest metal you are allowed to use is copper, which is useless for cutting stone. Instead, try this ancient Egyptian method. They inserted wooden wedges into cracks in the rock, and wet them. The wood expanded, splitting the rock evenly.

Step 3: You would now fill in the rest of your first layer.

Step 4: You would then use levers around a block of stone to lift it up gradually. Put layers of material underneath the gap to hold the block up. Then, when it has reached the height of the first layer, push the block into place. Now, the first block of your second stage is in place!

Step 5: Fill in the remaining blocks of your second stage. Only 199 more stages to go!

Step 6: Congratulations! Your pyramid should be about 164 yards high. (Check now — if it's not, you may have forgotten a layer.) Once all 2,500,000 stone blocks are in place, you will need to fill in the jagged sides so that the edges of your pyramid are smooth.

Step 7: Well done! You're finished. Stand back and admire the newest theme park attraction. Tell your workers that they can have the rest of the day off.

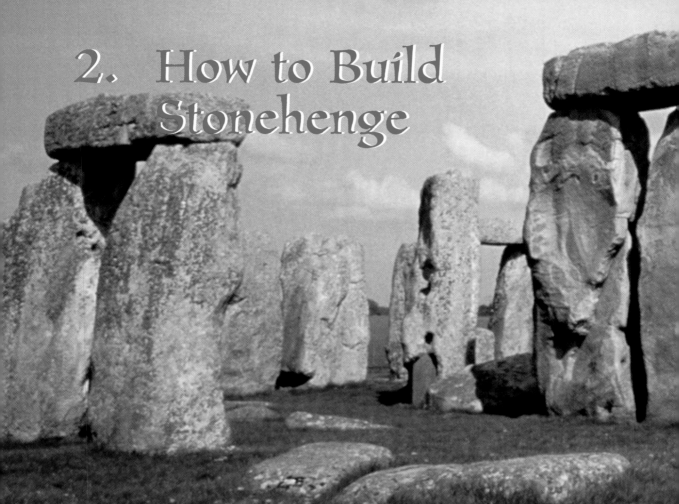

2. How to Build Stonehenge

The theme park company may not be keen on building a replica of the Great Pyramid, so read on to find out how to build Stonehenge using authentic materials, tools, and methods. Although it requires some accurate measuring and some huge, heavy blocks of stone, you'll find that a Stonehenge building project has a low difficulty rating.

Stonehenge's main stones have been carefully placed so that the sun shines through them on the shortest and longest days of the year. Your stones will have to be placed in the right position, too.

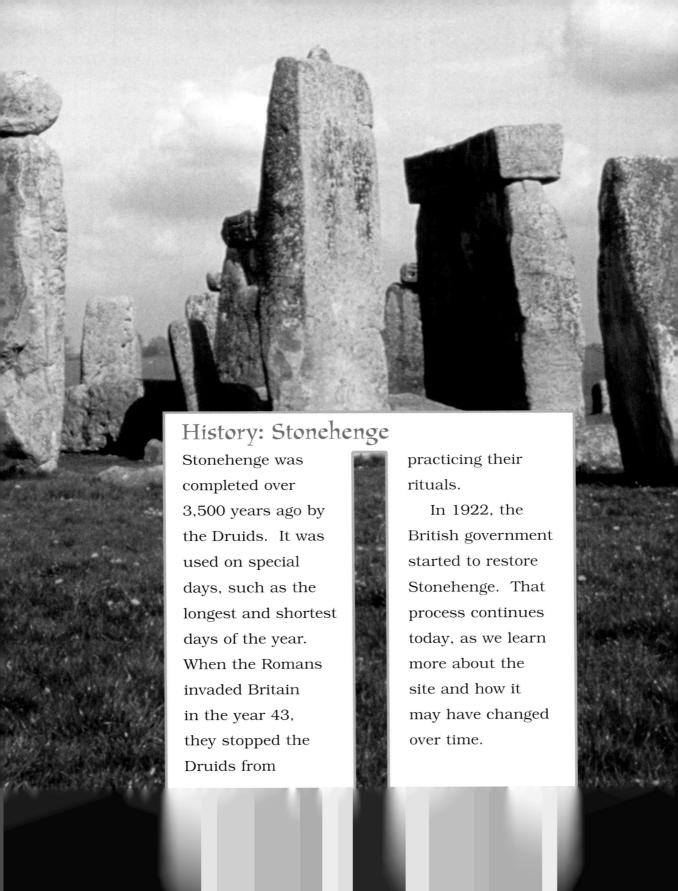

History: Stonehenge

Stonehenge was completed over 3,500 years ago by the Druids. It was used on special days, such as the longest and shortest days of the year. When the Romans invaded Britain in the year 43, they stopped the Druids from practicing their rituals.

In 1922, the British government started to restore Stonehenge. That process continues today, as we learn more about the site and how it may have changed over time.

What You Will Need

Location: For an authentic Stonehenge replica, you would find a high hilltop with good views of the horizon. Your theme park visitors will want to see the sun rising on the shortest and longest days of the year. A circular area, about 55 yards in diameter, would be fine.

Materials: You would need about 60 large rectangular blocks of sandstone, weighing between 26 and 40 tons each. As it would still be cheating to move your stones using vehicles with wheels, you would also need as much rope as you can find. Like the Druids, you would have to drag each rectangular block about 19 miles from the sandstone quarry.

You would also need 15 even larger bluestone blocks. Unfortunately, these will have to be brought from a quarry about 150 miles away. You should probably start thinking about how you will move these blocks now, as it will take you several years to get them in place!

Tools: To build a Stonehenge in the same way as the Druids, you would use some hard sharp stones, some bronze tools, and wooden implements.

Workers: You would need to hire thousands of workers to complete your Stonehenge. Most of them will be employed to maneuver the large blocks of stone from the quarries into your circle, but you will also need stonemasons, stone carvers, and astronomers.

Time: The Druids took about 1,000 years to complete Stonehenge — but you would probably skip Step 3, which took up 989 years. Instead, you should allow about ten years.

Who Were The Druids?

The Druids were Celts, members of a culture that once lived across Europe. Celts worshipped many gods and believed the plants mistletoe and oak to be sacred. In modern Europe, mistletoe is still used to decorate houses at certain times of the year, and oak trees are regarded as symbols of strength.

The Building Method

Step 1: You would start a replica of Stonehenge by building a large mound of earth.

Step 2: You would carefully observe where the sun rises on the longest day of the year. Then, after six months, observe where the sun rises on the shortest day of the year. Both places would be marked on the mound of earth. The bluestones would be carefully arranged pointing toward these spots.

Step 3: The Druids waited another 989 years before any more building. The theme park company would probably want you to work quicker!

Step 4: Next, you would mark out a circle around your bluestones and dig holes where the sandstone blocks would go. Make sure that one side of each hole has a sloping ramp!

Step 5: Your workers would lower the first sandstone block down the ramp. They would then slowly pull the side of the 40 ton block off the ramp into an upright position.

Step 6: Step 5 would be repeated another 29 times.

Step 7: You would carve grooves into the ends of the remaining sandstone blocks. Levers would be used to slowly lift them up to the top of the upright blocks. They would be placed in a continuous curve around the top of the circle.

Step 8: Congratulations! Your Stonehenge is finished. Now all you have to do is wait until the next longest or shortest day when you can celebrate!

Stone Astronomy

Stonehenge is one of many stone monuments built to act as a calendar or to observe the sun, moon, and stars. Many ancient Egyptian temples and pyramids are also aligned with stars. And, in America, early Native Americans laid out piles of stones to mark the position of sunrise and sunset on the longest day of the year.

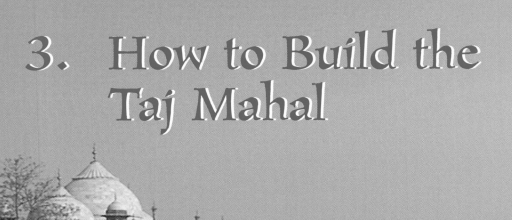

3. How to Build the Taj Mahal

To build replicas of the Great Pyramid and Stonehenge in the same way as the originals were built, you would need to rely on the strength of your builders and some very simple tools to work with the huge blocks of stone. For a replica of the Taj Mahal, you would need a different range of design and building skills and technology.

The Taj Mahal would be rated as a moderately difficult construction project. But it would be worth it! If you decided to build a replica of the Taj Mahal, you would be the envy of all the other theme parks in the world. Everyone would want their own Taj Mahal when they saw what your team had accomplished.

History: The Taj Mahal

In 1629, the emperor of India, Shah Jahan, was very excited. His wife, Mumtaz Mahal, was about to give birth to another baby. Unfortunately, his excitement turned to grief, as his wife died giving birth. Shah Jahan was so heartbroken that he decided to build the world's most beautiful building as a tomb for his dead wife.

Location: Before starting to build an authentic Taj Mahal, you would need to find a large, flat area with a river flowing nearby. A rectangular area, about 660 yards long and 330 yards wide, would be just right. An exact copy of the Taj Mahal would be over 66 yards tall, so the theme park company would have to make sure there were no rollercoasters or tall rides nearby!

Materials: You would need almost all the white marble that you could buy, along with 43 other different types of precious stones and thousands of jewels and gems.

Tools: You would need the best metal and wooden tools that you could find.

Workers: You would need to hire at least 20,000 workers to build a Taj Mahal in exactly the same way as the original. You would need stonemasons, stone carvers, sculptors, painters, craftspeople, jewelers, engineers, and gardeners.

Time: Using the same methods, a replica of the Taj Mahal would take about 22 years to complete — 11 years to finish the building and 11 years to landscape the grounds surrounding it.

Fine Art

The Taj Mahal has inspired artists for centuries. This photorealistic painting in oil by Vasili Vasileivich Vereshchagin is from about 1875. It hangs in the Tretyakov Gallery in Moscow.

The Building Method

Step 1: You would start by planning your building site. Your plan would include the Taj Mahal, several lakes, a large garden, an impressive gateway, some minarets, and a large wall to enclose the whole area.

Step 2: You would build four towers at each corner of your Taj Mahal.

Step 3: In between the four towers, you would build a huge room shaped like an octagon. The towers and the octagonal room would support the first dome of your Taj Mahal.

Step 4: Next, you would build your first dome between the four towers.

Step 5: On top of your first dome, you would build another. This one would be 20 yards in diameter and another 27 yards higher. It should curve outward, then inward, to give it a special shape.

Step 6: You would build four archways, 36 yards tall, one on each side of the Taj Mahal. Inside your replica of the Taj Mahal it would need to be decorated with thousands of intricately carved panels, inlaid with jewels and precious gems.

Step 7: You would fill the lakes, plant the gardens, and complete the wall. Then, you would have finished a copy of what many people agree is the world's most beautiful building.

Gateway

English artist Thomas Daniell created this view of the main gate and enclosing wall in 1796 as a color lithograph.

4. How to Build the Eiffel Tower

If your construction team can competently work with steel and iron, this replica building project would be ideal for them.

Imagine the views from the top of your authentic Eiffel Tower — soon after its completion, tourists will flock to your theme park!

History: The Eiffel Tower

The famous Eiffel Tower was built by Alexandre Gustave Eiffel. It was ready in 1889 to mark the 100th anniversary of the French revolution when France became a republic.

Alexandre Gustave Eiffel

(born 1832, died 1923)

Alexandre Gustave Eiffel was a French engineer who first became famous when he designed many railway bridges. Today, he is internationally known for his construction of the Eiffel Tower.

But did you know that in 1881, Eiffel's construction business helped to build the Statue of Liberty in Paris, France? Upon its completion, it was shipped in 214 cases to New York for reassembling. Looking formidable at over 160 yards high, the statue now stands on Ellis Island just off the coast of New York.

What You Will Need

Location: The great thing about an exact copy of the Eiffel Tower is that it could be built almost anywhere. All the steel girders would be assembled together elsewhere, so you wouldn't even need much room to work in!

Materials: You would need enough concrete to fill four large holes for the foundations, where each steel leg would sit.

In addition, you would need 12,000 steel girders of various lengths. To hold all the girders together, you would need 2.5 million rivets — but you should probably get a few extra. It's easy to accidentally drop one or two off the top of a tower, and they're very difficult to find later, especially in long grass!

Tools: You would use mostly modern tools, as well as cranes and plenty of scaffolding.

Workers: You would need to hire thousands of workers to complete an Eiffel Tower. Most of them would be employed to operate cranes and to join the steel girders together.

Time: Built in exactly the same way, a replica of the Eiffel Tower would take a little over two years to complete.

Concrete: Invented, Then Forgotten!

Concrete, which is used in almost all modern building projects, was first invented by the Romans 2,000 years ago. They mixed crushed limestone and volcanic ash together with water to form a concrete so strong that many Roman buildings and bridges survive today.

Amazingly, after the Roman empire was destroyed, people didn't continue using concrete. Most buildings were made from bricks, stones, plaster, or wood. It wasn't until 1,300 years after the end of the Roman empire, in 1756, that a British engineer called John Smeaton rediscovered how to make concrete!

The Building Method

Step 1: You would start by digging four holes at each corner of your site. You would then fill them with concrete.

Step 2: You would start building all four legs at the same time. Support each of them with a wooden frame until you are ready to build the first floor. This step takes about a year.

Step 3: You would put cranes on each leg to lift more and more steel girders above the first floor. Keep riveting the girders together, keeping them angled inwards, so the tower gets thinner at each stage!

Step 4: Once your tower has reached a height of 142 yards, you would build your second floor. This should only take four months.

Step 5: During the next nine months, you would keep building. Remember to leave plenty of open spaces between the girders so strong winds can pass through easily. The theme park company will not want their Eiffel Tower to blow over!

Step 6: You would put a weather station and a radio transmitter on the top.

Step 7: Congratulations! Your Eiffel Tower is now finished. Enjoy the view!

Iron And Steel

Since prehistoric times, people have known how to melt down rocks containing iron to extract the metal in molten form. But it wasn't until the mid-1800s that the stronger, purer form of iron we call steel could be made.

In 1857, metallurgists (scientists who study metals) discovered that by adding the chemicals carbon, manganese, and oxygen to molten iron, they could easily make large quantities of steel. The Eiffel Tower was one of the first structures made mainly from steel, and it proved that steel could be used safely and efficiently in buildings.

5. How to Build the Forth Bridge

Transportation structures, such as bridges and in particular railway bridges, have always held an important and essential role throughout the world. Build a railway bridge based on the Forth Bridge in South Queensferry, Scotland, and you will impress all who visit your theme park.

With a medium to high difficulty rating, you would use a variety of materials, such as iron, steel, and concrete to build a replica of the bridge.

History: The Forth Bridge

In the 19th century, many railways were built to transport people and goods quickly and safely over long distances. The presence of rivers initiated the building of many railway bridges, and this was also the case in Scotland where steam engines needed to cross some large, wide rivers.

At 570 yards long, the construction of the Forth Bridge took eight years. It was finally completed in 1890.

Bridge Technology

First known
stone bridge
2,200 BC

Roman bridges
use concrete
10 BC

First iron
bridge
1790

First steel
cable bridge
1955

Some Famous Bridge Designs

Forth Bridge,
Scotland
1890

London Tower
Bridge, England
1894

Sydney Harbor
Bridge, Australia
1932

Golden Gate
Bridge, USA
1937

Location: Even with the best technology available, some rivers are just too wide to build a single span across. If you were still at the low difficulty level, you'd find this was a real nuisance. And if you want to build foundations in the middle of the river, you will have to dig down three times as deep as the river itself. It would be impossible! Instead, to build a replica of the Forth Bridge, you would want to choose a place where a small island has formed in the middle of a river. You would use the island to put a central support on.

Materials: To build an exact replica, you would need about 58,000 tons of steel. The steel tubes would need to be 13 feet wide to build your main supports. You would need enough concrete to fill three huge holes, 29.5 yards deep.

Tools: You would use steam engines, nuts, bolts, rivets, and modern metal tools.

Workers: You would need to hire thousands of workers to build your bridge. Most of them would be steel workers.

Time: Using the original methods, your bridge would be completed in about eight years.

A Beautiful Design, A Terrible Purpose

Amongst the many beautifully designed buildings and bridges of Venice, in Italy, is a tiny bridge called the "Bridge of Sighs." The people of Venice gave the bridge its name because it leads from the main palace in Venice to the dungeons where prisoners were executed. Prisoners crossing the bridge "sighed" because they knew they would not be coming back again!

The Building Method

Step 1: You would start by digging three huge holes, called caissons, for the bridge supports. The holes need to be 29.5 yards deep. When they are dug, you would fill them with concrete.

Step 2: You would start building your support towers out of steel tubes. They would be 109 yards high, over 438 yards long, and 40 yards wide at the base.

Step 3: When the ends of your towers have met, you would join them together. Now you have a bridge over half a mile long! You would add a railway track through the middle, and start painting the steel. If you started at one end, by the time you finished, you would have to start repainting the bridge!

The Golden Gate Bridge

The Golden Gate Bridge in San Francisco is one of the world's largest suspension bridges. Its six-lane road is held above the water by two steel cables. Each cable is made up of 27,752 thinner wires, which took six years to spin together while the bridge was being built.

6. How to Build the Empire State Building

Although the 102-story Empire State Building is no longer the world's tallest building, the New York building is probably one of the best known skyscrapers. If you want to build something quickly for the theme park, then an Empire State Building is worth considering. Started in March 1930, the whole building was finished by the end of 1931, costing $25 million! In one ten-day period, workers managed to build 14 storys on top of the building — that's fast work!

At the same time as the Empire State Building was being built, another skyscraper, the Chrysler Building, was being built a few blocks away. The builders of the Empire State Building were horrified to see that it was almost as tall as their building — so they added another 65.5 yards to the Empire State, just to make sure it was the world's tallest at that time!

If you want to build an Empire State Building, you should be careful where you build it. The real Empire State Building is so tall that flocks of migrating birds often hit it as they fly south for the winter. And, in 1945, on a foggy morning, an airplane crashed right into the 79th floor!

Location: Skyscrapers are best built where land is expensive. A replica of the Empire State Building would need about 2.5 acres of land for its base — and you'll need lots of solid granite underneath the land to support the building — skyscrapers are heavy!

Materials: You would need 66,000 tons of steel frame, 10 million bricks, 70 miles of water pipe, 50 miles of radiators for heating, 1056 miles of telephone cable, and 6500 windows. Plus, you would need 18 truckloads of elevator parts to be delivered each day, to build 73 elevators. You would also need to buy a whole quarry in Europe, so the marble you use in the foyers looks the same throughout the building!

Tools: You would need cranes, and plenty of tools to weld and rivet steel frames together.

Workers: You would need 4000 workers to complete an Empire State Building, and they would work for a total of 7 million working hours! Luckily, the steel workers would only be paid $200 each month, using 1930 wages.

KING KONG!

Movie Madness

The Empire State Building was built in an unfashionable part of New York. At first, people didn't want to rent offices in it. But, when the movie *King Kong* was released in the 1930s, it became very popular. In the movie, a giant gorilla climbs up the outside of the building after capturing a woman, while fighting off airplanes at the same time!

The Building Method

Step 1: One of the problems when building skyscrapers in busy cities is that there is nowhere to store huge amounts of steel, bricks, and concrete. To build a replica in exactly the same way as the original, the building materials you need each day must be brought to your site each morning! You can't have all the materials listed on page 28 arriving at once!

Step 2: You would dig out the soil from your 2.5 acre block until you reached solid granite, almost 22 yards below ground level. There, you would start to build the foundations.

Step 3: In Pittsburgh, 397 miles away from New York, a huge steel factory made prefabricated steel frames, each weighing 44 tons. The frames were then transported to the New York building site and joined together like gigantic toy blocks. You would need to do the same by building a miniature railway on each story to move the steel frames around.

Step 4: When you finished the steel frame for one story, you would simply climb up to the top, and start another story. Following this stage, other workers below would fill in the spaces with bricks and windows!

Step 5: You would repeat steps 3 and 4 about $4\frac{1}{2}$ times each week.

Step 6: After repeating the process 102 times you're ready to admire the view from the observation deck at the top. On a clear day, you would be able to see for 75 miles!

But wait — don't stand too far back! Oops.

Skywalkers

Many young Mohawk Indians, from Canada and the USA, were employed to work in the highest, most dangerous places on the Empire State Building. They called themselves *skywalkers*. The young Mohawk Indians believed that being able to work at high altitudes meant they had come of age, or were truly a brave adult.

Modern Architecture: The Sydney Opera House

In 1955 a competition was held in Australia to design a new opera house in Sydney, and to most people's surprise, the competition was won by a little-known Danish architect called Jørn Utzon. He created the unique "shell" shape that is now recognized as a world landmark and has come to symbolize Australia.

The Sydney Opera House has over 1,000 rooms, and 11 acres of floor space. The shells are covered in ceramic tiles, a building material which has been used since ancient times. Utzon chose ceramic tiles because he wanted a material that would gleam in the sun, survive temperature changes, keep itself clean, and look good for many years. In total, the entire roof of the Sydney Opera House contains 1,056,000 individual tiles.

Building began in 1959, but the building was not finished until 1973 — 14 years later, and at a total cost of A$102 million.

Conclusion

You've now completed your imaginary trip around the world. Knowing what people, resources, materials, tools, and methods you need to build an authentic copy of each of the building projects, which one will you recommend to the theme park company? Which one will be the most popular for visitors to come and see? Which one will be the easiest to build? Which one will be the hardest? Which one can be built for under 500 million dollars? Which one, out of all the projects you have seen, will get the stamp of approval?

Project Manager's Recommendation for New Theme Park Attraction:

The Great Pyramid ☐

Stonehenge ☐

Taj Mahal ☐ **APPROVED**

Eiffel Tower ☐

Forth Bridge ☐

Empire State Building ☐

Estimated Cost: ....

Estimated Building Time: ....

Index

Bookweb Links

More Bookweb books about
creative achievements:

Meet the Artists — Nonfiction
The Dragon Compass — Fiction
The Magnificent Mural — Fiction
Virtual Reality — Fiction

Key to Bookweb
Fact Boxes
☐ Arts
☐ Health
☐ Science
☐ Social Studies
☐ Technology